ASPERGER
MEETS
GIRL

of related interest

Asperger Syndrome – A Love Story
Sarah Hendrickx and Keith Newton
Foreword by Tony Attwood
ISBN 978 1 84310 540 4

Alone Together
Making an Asperger Marriage Work
Katrin Bentley
Foreword by Tony Attwood
ISBN 978 1 84310 537 4

Aspergers in Love
Maxine Aston
Foreword by Gisela Slater-Walker
ISBN 978 1 84310 115 4

An Asperger Marriage
Gisela and Christopher Slater-Walker
Foreword by Tony Attwood
ISBN 978 1 84310 017 1

Asperger Syndrome and Long-Term Relationships
Ashley Stanford
Foreword by Liane Holliday Willey
ISBN 978 1 84310 734 7

Sex, Sexuality and the Autism Spectrum
Wendy Lawson
Foreword by Glenys Jones
ISBN 978 1 84310 284 7

The Complete Guide to Asperger's Syndrome
Tony Attwood
ISBN 978 1 84310 495 7

ASPERGER MEETS GIRL

Happy Endings for Asperger Boys

JONATHAN GRIFFITHS

Foreword by Hugh Jones

Jessica Kingsley Publishers
London and Philadelphia

First published in 2008
by Jessica Kingsley Publishers
116 Pentonville Road
London N1 9JB, UK
and
400 Market Street, Suite 400
Philadelphia, PA 19106, USA

www.jkp.com

Library of Congress Cataloging in Publication Data
Griffiths, Jonathan, 1968-
    Asperger meets girl : happy endings for Asperger boys / Jonathan Griffiths ; foreword by
Hugh Jones.
        p. cm.
    ISBN 978-1-84310-630-2 (pb : alk. paper) 1. Asperger's syndrome--Patients--Sexual
behavior. 2. Asperger's syndrome--Social aspects. I. Title.
    RC553.A88G746 2008
    362.196'858832--dc22

                                                                    2007035090

British Library Cataloguing in Publication Data
A CIP catalogue record for this book is available from the British Library

ISBN 978 1 84310 630 2

Printed and bound in Great Britain by
Athenaeum Press, Gateshead, Tyne and Wear

Note

The material in this book was first published in 2005 under the title *Sex Tips for Sad
Bastards* by pertinax@thesadbastard.com, and distributed through the website
www.thesadbastard.com, where related material can still be found and discussed.

CONTENTS

FOREWORD

Nerds, by and large, like games. Games have rules, and rules can be analysed and understood. It doesn't really matter whether the game in question is chess or dungeons and dragons – wherever games are played, nerds can be found playing them, enthusiastically, obsessively even, and usually successfully.

There is one game, though, at which nerds (forgive me) suck, and which they typically lose. I mean, of course, the mating game, that strange struggle to acquire and retain a sexual partner and companion. This game is bewildering to the average nerd. He knows that games are one of his strong points, but the interpersonal behaviour of the non-nerd populace doesn't resemble, to him, any other game that he knows. There don't appear to be any rules. The conditions for victory vary from case to case. What works for one guy with one girl doesn't work with any other pairing. Language develops a disturbingly imprecise connection with meaning. After a few failures, many nerds simply give up and return to the chess board.

It is becoming increasingly clear to scientists that the reason for these difficulties is that nerds are, to a greater or lesser extent, 'mind blind'. Other people baffle them. They find it difficult to work out what other people are feeling and thinking. They seem unaware of body language and other subtle signals about another person's inner state. Rejection, when it seemingly inevitably arrives, comes out of the blue, and yet from the point of view of the person doing the rejection, it is the culmination of repeated hints and warnings.

Mind blindness is now recognised as a cardinal feature of Autism Spectrum Disorders (ASDs). Asperger's Syndrome (AS) is one such disorder, and it is now clear that its prevalence is far greater than was once thought. This is partly because the mind blindness of people with Asperger's may be far from obvious. They may seem weird, or rude, but not obviously disabled. They may have some rewarding relationships, especially with people who are aware of their difficulties and have learned to make adjustments. Nonetheless, when you look more closely you discover someone who finds the behaviour of other people frightening and bewildering, their motives and feelings opaque. This comparatively mild form of mind blindness makes forming new relationships, especially sexual relationships, at best a difficult and confusing process. Of course, it isn't only people who've been diagnosed with an ASD who experience these kinds of difficulty. The term 'nerd' is used here (entirely non-pejoratively) to include all those people who find the whole world of interpersonal relationships deeply baffling, who experience any degree of mind blindness.

Asperger's Syndrome is overwhelmingly more common in men than in women, which fact I plead in defence of my gender-specific pronouns earlier on. Nerds, as well as people with AS, are typically men who are drawn to closed systems: railway timetables; games; computer programming; dead languages; pure mathematics. Nerds like to immerse themselves in worlds that are wholly susceptible to logical analysis. They like to know the rules. If you know the rules, you can work out what is going to happen, you can win the game.

So far, not much hope for our nerd who wants to try his hand at the mating game. But help is at hand in the form of this remarkable book. Its author, a self-confessed nerd himself, came to the realisation many years ago that the reason he was losing the game was that other people possessed information that he was unable to access. The ability to see into other people's heads, to read people's body language correctly, to know without being told in unromantically precise terms whether someone fancied him or not, was an ability he didn't have, and probably wouldn't ever have. That vital database was barred, the password hardwired into the brains of others, but not his. And in the context of this devastating news, well-meant advice about 'being yourself' and 'relaxing' and 'making eye contact' and 'smiling' (some of this advice being given by me, I'm sorry to say) only resulted in making him look even weirder.

Lesser mortals would have given up. But our intrepid author decided to work on the hypothesis that the mating game was just that, a game. And if it was a game, it ought to be possible to work out what the rules were. And if one knew the rules, one could find a way to play it that didn't rely on the intuitions others take for granted. And if one could do that, one might just, one day, if all went well, and one kept to one's game plan, maybe, end up getting laid.

The author did better than that. He married a beautiful and brilliant Australian concert pianist, and is now father of two beautiful and brilliant girls. The transformation from über-nerd to alpha male took me, and most of his friends, by surprise. Were he less generous of spirit, I would imagine he would want to keep his secrets to himself. Thankfully, he hasn't. In these covers the rules of the game are explained, not in the opaque language only accessible to non-nerds, but in straightforward, precise, and often extremely funny prose. This book is a gift to all nerds. There is, after all, hope.

Hugh Jones, MA (Psychology)
D.Phil (Developmental Psychology)

PREFACE

The author has no doctorate in transactional analysis and no thriving counselling practice. He is totally unqualified to write on this subject, except for this one vital qualification: that it takes one to know one.

He designs software for a living, and had no girlfriend until the age of 22, but is now married to a beautiful Australian. His father used to be a trainspotter, so his very existence just goes to show that there's hope for us all.

1 WHAT PROBLEM AM I TRYING TO SOLVE HERE?

Well, here you are, either with a bright shiny diagnosis of Asperger's Syndrome or a murky collection of Asperger-like problems to a 'subclinical' degree. In either case, I hope you won't be offended if I address you as a fellow nerd. A spade is a spade, and a nerd is a nerd.

Let's suppose you function adequately from one day to the next (give or take, perhaps, the odd nervous break-down). However, your life is not yet enriched by the delight and inspiration that can come from an intimate personal relationship. And you can't get laid.

You and I were off sick from school the day they explained how to flirt. One day, we looked around, and everyone else knew how to do it. How did they know? It was a mystery.

Of course, it doesn't really happen like that; everyone has to go through a learning process, which is usually embarrassing. But it is still different for us nerds. One difference is that it's a much, much longer learning process. Another is that it's hard for us even to start this process.

We could live with a bit of trial and error, if only we had some clue as to what trials we might try. The thing is, to take any kind of action, we nerds need methods, of the kind that can be communicated in words or formal symbols.

Unfortunately, the nerd-taking-advice-in-hopes-to-get-the-girl is a stock figure in comedy right back to Shakespeare, and probably beyond. We know from experience that if we rely on the methods of those people to whom it all comes naturally, then the joke is on us.

Instead, we need our own nerdy solutions to our own nerdy problems. We need a kind of romance with the logical unity and clarity of a formal software specification, or of a well-elaborated metaphysical system.

To that end, this book offers two things. One is a structured conceptual model for interpreting courtship and sexual behaviour so that it can be understood by us anoraks who have no instinct for this stuff. The other is some advice. This 'advice' bit leans heavily on my own experience, but I believe there are other men and boys out there with whom it will strike a chord. I hope you find it helpful. Failing that, I hope it gives you a good laugh.

2 A NERD'S EYE VIEW OF HUMAN SEXUALITY

We nerds can understand abstract models of things. In this chapter there are three ideas you can use for modelling human sexual behaviour. Some might say that no abstract model could properly reflect the infinite variety of love and desire, etc. Fair enough, but if you're the sort of person who needs to understand things at an abstract level, then an imperfect model is better than none, if only because of the confidence it gives you.

They may not capture every aspect of the subject, but I've found these ideas useful for turning all those nudges, winks and unspoken things that 'everyone knows' into something intelligible.

2.1 Idea 1: The space of possibilities
Sexuality can be considered under three headings.

One heading is about sensuality. I'm talking about the pleasures of touch, and scent and taste. (Easy, tiger!)

Another is about attention. This works two ways. It includes the pleasures of having someone's undivided attention, and it includes the pleasures of paying attention, of gazing at someone and of knowing where they are and what they're doing in every waking moment. 'Intimacy' might be the best one-word label for this heading, although some might object that intimacy is something that you only achieve *after* you've put in some 'paying attention' work.

The third heading is about power relations. This works two ways too. It includes the pleasure of dominating and the pleasure of being dominated. You can see its unacceptable face on prostitutes' cards in the phone boxes of London, but it comes out in subtler ways elsewhere.

If you find it helpful, you could think of these three 'headings' as three axes on a Cartesian diagram: hence the term 'space of possibilities'. If you don't, that's okay too; we can work around that.

(*Psst*: if you like Cartesian diagrams, there are some explicit illustrations of this space in the Appendix.)

2.1.1 Plotting some points in the space

Coming up next are some examples of how to use the three-heading idea to interpret situations. I'll have to go out on a limb here because there's never going to be a formal interpretation of the sexual content of a situation that can't be disputed. However, the idea is just to show the sort of way that you can use the structure I'm offering, and not to be too dogmatic about any particular case.

Because this is a book, not a video, I can't give you fly-on-the-wall examples with real-time commentary. Instead, I'll quote some extracts from fiction and apply the three-heading idea to *them*. That means categorising the feelings of characters under these headings. We'll be revisiting the same extracts later to illustrate the use of the other two ideas.

Some of these extracts look at the situation from a man's point of view and some from a woman's. Before we go any further, you may be wondering why I'm quoting things which are really about men's feelings about women, whereas the mystery you need explained is that of women's feelings about men.

Well, at the level of this three-heading idea, those two things are not so different. I don't hold with the idea that 'women are from Venus' or any other extraterrestrial location. On the contrary my experience, such as it is, has taught me that you can find parallels between your sexuality and her sexuality, and when you find them they can bring the two of you together in very satisfactory ways, of which more later.

Anyway, on with the extracts.

2.1.2 Old-fashioned romance

Here's a passage from Tolstoy's nineteenth-century classic *Anna Karenina*, in which an earnest gentleman called Levin is having a disagreement with an adulterous friend:

> Well, you must excuse me there. You know I separate women into two categories at least, no it would be truer to say: there are women and there are... I have never seen, nor ever shall see, a fallen woman who was exquisite. (Tolstoy 1878)

Here's another passage in which the 'fallen woman' that the novel is all about meets her future lover Vronsky:

> As he looked round, she too turned her head. Her brilliant grey eyes, shadowed by thick lashes, gave him a friendly, attentive look, as though she were recognising him, and then turned to the approaching crowd as if in search of someone. In that brief glance Vronsky had time to notice the suppressed animation which played over her face and flitted between her sparkling eyes and the slight smile curving her red lips. It was as though her nature were so brimming over with something that against her will it expressed itself now in a radiant look, now in a smile. (Tolstoy 1878)

So, what's going on in these two passages?

1. **Sensuality**: this being the nineteenth century, the closest we get to sensuality in either passage is an explicit reference to eyelashes.

2. **Intimacy**: the second passage (the description of Anna) is big on attention, as suggested by eye contact. We've got 'brilliant grey eyes', 'a friendly, attentive look', 'sparkling eyes' and 'a radiant look'.

3. **Power**: in the same passage we've also got suggestions of power – 'suppressed animation' and 'nature brimming over'. You might argue that, if Anna were really sexually powerful, then the animation wouldn't be suppressed. Well, the plot of the novel is driven largely by the breakdown of that suppression, as Anna embarks on her affair and takes the consequences.

What about the first passage? What can we say about Levin's view? Let's say that a 'fallen woman' is any woman who is conscious of her sexuality and doesn't confine it to one private relationship. I suppose Levin is uncomfortable with the power of conscious sexuality in a woman. The conventional feminist reading of this is that some men just don't like women to have any power at all, but I think a more specific explanation is possible in this case. You see, Levin himself is a bit of a nerd. He's awkward. He is handicapped by weak social skills. He makes great efforts to understand how the world works, and to do the right thing in it, but a sexually confident woman would confront him with a world that makes no sense to him. He just couldn't read her. He wouldn't know what to do for the best.

Anyway, what about this 'exquisite' that a 'fallen woman' can never be? Unfortunately 'exquisite' is the sort of word that can be applied to collectibles. That's a bit hard on Levin personally, but it's fair to say that if you love to look at 'exquisite' things, they're the kind of things that don't stare back at you. So he wants someone to lavish attention on. If he dares to think at all about a sensual relationship or a power relationship with a woman, these thoughts aren't colouring his vocabulary.

To summarise, we've got one character, Anna, who likes giving attention and exerting power, and another character, Levin, who also likes giving attention.

2.1.3 Swinging

This one's from the 1960s, in a novel by Peter De Vries about a famous (fictional) poet called Gowan McGland:

In a spasm of rage and despair he remembered he would be toothless by forty. There was only and always one cure for this now: reach out for any woman his widening vogue made available to him and clasp her like a poultice to his abscessed heart. It was what his henceforth Gargantuan philandering amounted to – slaking in as many arms as possible the thirst for reassurance in the race with Time.

He had seen the girl in the blue wool dress note his arrival at the party...and when she said, 'Aren't you Gowan McGland?' he knew only too well what she meant. She meant, 'My God, are *you* Gowan McGland?'...'Guilty,' he said, taking in her not very shapely but probably cozy body. She was a foot too short and round as a cheese, but he was no prize either.

After the first compliments about his latest group, as well as some elucidations by the girl of meanings in them McGland had not suspected, they fell silent, watching the growing jam of guests.

[There's a professional rival of McGland's at the party, and the girl claims that he, the rival, is homosexual, and that his poetry is no good.]

They left for his flat shortly after midnight.

'I particularly like the one that goes, "The Lord my God has widgeons in his hair,"' she said as she peeled a stocking from a fat thigh. McGland nodded from the pillow. The sensation was beginning to come over him that he experienced when having something demonstrated to him that he had no intention of buying. One was not merely wicked, debauched and depraved – one was naughty. Released from their supports her breasts dropped like hanged men. The rest of her sprang free of its elastic prison, and she was in beside him, warm and cold both, and thrillingly clammy. (Excerpt from: *Reuben Reuben* by Peter De Vries 1984. Copyright © Derek and Jonathan De Vries.)

Like Levin, poor old McGland is interested in **attention**, but he's interested in having women lavish it on him, not the other way round. Also, he clearly appreciates **sensuality**. The cosiness of a girl's body is more important to him than its shapeliness. Sensible man.

But what does the girl in the blue dress find to appreciate in him? Well, maybe the two of them are quite alike in being grateful for whatever clammy sensual comfort they can get. However, for the girl, there's the added factor that he's famous. I'm not sure, but I think we file this under **power**. It's stretching a point in the case of Gowan McGland, but I think we can live with that.

To summarise, we've got a character who likes sensuality and receiving attention and another character who likes experiencing power in her lover and giving him attention.

2.1.4 Student fantasy

This is from an early 1990s poem, 'Sugar-lips', by a literature student, Vesna McMaster:

> As he watched, his brow became lumpy, and his throat jumped
> Backwards. She flayed the cherry with her teeth, then
> Slowly dipped the carcass in fine white sugar.
> Her red lips opened on him: honey flowed out and filled the room.
> As he felt the rest of the earth stagger and fall,
> Her eyes shot him, casually. Then she ate another cherry. (McMaster 1993)

This is about a woman receiving **attention** and exerting **power** and indulging herself **sensually** in a sugared cherry, all at once. Ooh, yeah.

2.1.5 Coming up roses

This extract is from *Getting Personal* by Chris Manby. It's what's called 'chick lit' and describes dating in 2002. Here, the female protagonist, Ruby, goes on a blind date:

'I must not get too excited. I must not get too excited.'…It isn't him after all. Or if it is him, he doesn't fancy me. He's the wrong man. Or he's going to pretend I've got the wrong man because I'm clearly not the right sort of woman. There must be some other guy with serial killer hair waiting for me round the corner. A guy this good-looking isn't going to…

'Ruby!' She had almost turned to go when Robert suddenly seized her hand and planted a smacker on the back of it. The thin line of his mouth was now an extravagant upward curve… He handed her the roses. And though she had been expecting to see a man waiting for her with a bunch of flowers, Ruby found she was suddenly inordinately thrilled. Not just one dozen red roses but two dozen. And not the kind of petal-bare bunches you find at the supermarket wrapped in a triangle of cellophane, either. The roses were wrapped in gloriously crunchy brown paper and tied in Raffia – the Knightsbridge version of clear plastic wrap… Ruby felt herself physically open out like the buds she held in her hand. As he complimented her on the beige raincoat she had bought five years previously, she was sure she felt herself grow a whole inch taller in the warmth of his gentle flattery. When he told her that he had noticed her walking towards him and didn't dare think that she might be the girl he was looking for because she was so scrumptious, Ruby felt her face glow… When Robert grinned at her, she knew her eyes were twinkling almost as much as his. By the time they got to the restaurant, she had counted at least half a dozen girls looking enviously in her direction. She felt as though she had undergone a Hollywood makeover in the ten-minute walk from the tube station to the trendy, minimalist restaurant where Robert had booked a table. (Excerpt from: *Getting Personal* by Chris Manby. Copyright © 2004 Chris Manby. Reproduced by permission of Hodder and Stoughton Limited. This edition published by arrangement with Harlequin Books S.A. All rights reserved (Manby 2004)

Once she knows that her blind date really is hers, Ruby's immediate focus is on the **sensuality** of roses, petal and bud, but there's other stuff going on here as well. In addition to **attention** from Robert (in the form of flattery), Ruby is getting envious attention from half a dozen girls, which is very much part of her enjoyment of her situation. The element of **power** here is much less obvious. Essentially, it's mediated through shopping. Whereas, in *Anna Karenina*, Vronsky's power-attraction lay in his military bearing and physique, his rank and his sword, Robert's power here is consumer power. He drives a Porsche (not in this excerpt, but elsewhere) and shops in the right places (Knightsbridge).

We don't really get Robert's side of this whole experience. Because he turns out (later) to be a shallow scumbag, I suppose the author didn't want to invest much sympathy in him; he exists as a superficially attractive phantasm to distract the heroine from her ultimate soulmate.

2.1.6 *Slippery when wet*

This is a separate excerpt from the same novel. This time, the male protagonist, Martin, has the blind date:

'Scratch the surface and they're all the same,' Cindy yawned. 'Trustafarians the lot of them.'

'Oh,' said Martin.

'Bankrolled by their mummies and daddies. I thought it would be more unusual to go out with someone *ordinary*,' said Cindy, rubbing her fingers over the knot at the top of Martin's tie. 'I thought, how about going for someone who doesn't pretend he's got a creative bone in his body? Someone who has to advertise for a date because he's so boring? Someone who'll be so bloody grateful to have met me that he'll simply have to show me a damn good time.'...'My place,' she growled at him, then moved swiftly back to the business of sticking her slippery tongue down his throat... He didn't have a chance to get a word out all the way back to Cindy's house... [She handcuffs him to a towel rail and puts on music.]

'Cindy,' Martin called, 'you're not seriously going to play that are you? There's no way I can get down to it to a soundtrack by that bunch of nancy-boys.'

'Silence, slave!'

'What?'

'I said silence!'

Cindy reappeared in the doorway. She wasn't naked anymore. Oh no. She was wearing a black cat mask and a matching leather bikini. In her right hand she held a long leather bullwhip. In her left, a huge purple vibrator. Her nipples poked through slits in the bikini cups. Martin's first instinct was to laugh... 'I'm role-playing,' Cindy explained patiently... Take That on repeat. A tepid shower. And a barking mad rich girl prancing about the bathroom... Sod this, thought Martin. Not even he was this desperate to get laid. (Excerpts from: *Getting Personal* by Chris Manby. Copyright © 2004 Chris Manby. Reproduced by permission of Hodder and Stoughton Limited. This edition published by arrangement with Harlequin Books S.A. All rights reserved.)

There's a nod to **sensuality** here in the tongue action and some fancy fingering (most of which I've cut for brevity), but it soon becomes apparent that, for Cindy at least, the real interest is in **power**. She makes it clear early on that she's picked an inferior as her date. She also makes it clear that she's done this so as to get more of his **attention** than she gets from her peers. She uses sensuality to get Martin into her power, and then she uses that power to demand his attention to her 'prancing around'.

In this excerpt, unlike the last, we do get some of the man's point of view (because the man in question is the male lead). We learn that he is desperate, but mostly we learn that he can be led by the penis through the mechanism of basic, easy sensuality, and only considerable physical discomfort enables him to think at any other level.

Evidence elsewhere in the novel suggests that Cindy is the novelist's idea of what men, in general, want (minus the handcuffs, perhaps). Martin subsequently has a substantially happy sexual relationship with Cindy, ended by two things: one is the maturing realisation that this relationship is socially empty (no friendship involved, basically) and the other is the fact that Cindy's attention span is exhausted and she moves on.

2.2 Idea 2: The conventional games

So we've done Idea 1, then. Using Idea 1, we can develop a second idea that gives us some clues to the social rules that affect people's sexual behaviour.

What do people actually do in this 'space of possibilities' described by Idea 1? Very often, what they do is play games.

These games have rules, which most people 'pick up' from their friends and family by some sort of instinct, without really having to think about them. Unfortunately, one of the defining characteristics of a nerd is that he doesn't have this sort of instinct. We nerds need these games and rules spelt out for us. This section spells out some of them. It isn't possible to spell out *all* the rules, and in fact, if it ever looked as though we nerds were close to learning all the rules, then those other bastards would just go and change them. However, some guidelines are better than none, so here goes.

2.2.1 The conventional male game

If you listen to a group of men talking about sex, you often get the impression that they go out there to impress their mates. There's a sexual boasting game going on within the male gender that's all about which man's the *man*.

The conventional male game is about making sexual conquests. You score points in this game by 'scoring', and you get more points for a girl that makes all your mates jealous than for one you just happen to like yourself; that shows you're more powerful than them. Also, you score more points for a girl who's hard to get, or reluctant. That shows you're more powerful than *her*. If she's a virgin and you get there first, then you've scored both ways: you won the race against other men, and you overcame her presumed reservations.

In terms of our 'space of possibilities', it's all about the **power relations** aspect of sexuality.

2.2.2 The conventional female game

Women traditionally play a different game. I stress 'traditionally', because this is very much subject to change at the moment. The traditional woman's game is about her being more confident, desirable and admired than her peers without being too obviously sexually inviting.

Whereas men aim to be at the top, women aim to be at the centre.

Evidence? Recently an intelligent teenage girl, eager to be a 'success' in life, rattled off to a journalist a list of women she considered 'successful'. They were all famous for appearing on screen, and little else. Powerful-but-less-televised women did not feature in this list.

For contrast, consider that archetype of old-fashioned Western masculinity, Clint Eastwood's 'Man with No Name' character. He's powerful. He defeats his enemies and achieves his goals. Few women want to be like that though, because no one knows who he is – 'no name', remember?

In the terms of Idea 1, the conventional female game is all about getting **attention** without giving **sensuality**. Why not giving sensuality? Well, you'd be devaluing that currency which all women have to spend.

Of course, now that women have access to other kinds of currency, such as the pound sterling, this isn't nearly so important but old habits die hard. Even a girl who likes girl power can still call other girls 'sluts' or 'slags'. Also, not everything changes; there's more sensuality around than there used to be, but not less attention seeking.

2.2.3 And?

How does this stuff help us?

Well, when a boy and a girl first meet, their behaviour is often driven more by the intra-gender games they've each played with their friends than by their authentic feelings about each other. Being aware of these games confers a number of benefits.

2.2.3.1 LIBERATION

Once you understand the patterns that seem to govern courtship behaviour, you can free yourself from them. This sounds rather ambitious, but it's just a matter of asking yourself, 'Do I need to play this male status game about conquests, or is it more important just to get a woman I like?' Once you've observed that the rules of this game were not laid down by God Almighty, and that they work only to other men's advantage at your expense, it's not difficult to decide to bypass them.

2.2.3.2 CONFIDENCE

Knowing that these games are going on is not the same as knowing what the score is at any given moment; to know that, you need the sharp non-verbal communication skills that we nerds find so hard. However, if you can even make an educated guess at what might be going on in a social situation, that helps. It helps you to focus on the people around you, which in itself makes you less self-conscious. Being less self-conscious makes you less prone to embarrassment, and it stops you from radiating those non-verbal panic signals to which we nerds are prone on those occasions when we just don't get it.

2.2.3.3 A WINDOW OF OPPORTUNITY

During the past hundred years or so, women have learned men's tricks and men have, by and large, failed to learn women's tricks. Those men who *have* shown any propensity to learn women's tricks have been labelled as gay, and have, by and large, accepted that label.

What this means is that there are women who can admit to enjoying sensuality more than men, and who don't want to be either easy 'conquests' or chaste and unattainable, and there aren't (yet) enough men out there who can deal with them on those terms. What *that* means is, if you can adapt yourself to the sexuality of those women, then the law of supply and demand will start working in your favour. And you can adapt yourself, once you've seen how arbitrary and mutable the existing situation is.

Update: in more recent years, the phenomenon of the 'metrosexual' has emerged; the heterosexual man who grooms. You could see this phenomenon as a response to precisely the opportunity I described here. Don't worry though. This doesn't mean you've missed the bus. At worst, it means that you'll have to do more of your own analysis in order to spot the latest opportunities, but you can still use the same analytical tools.

2.2.4 Revisiting the extracts

Who's following the conventional rules in our literary extracts, and who's breaking them? And why? And with what consequences for nerds?

2.2.4.1 OLD-FASHIONED ROMANCE II

In the milieu of Anna Karenina, the brutishness of the conventional male game is sometimes tempered by good manners. Levin's adulterous friend would not positively boast about his adultery, and would certainly not draw attention to the fact that he is enjoying two relationships while Levin has none. That was then, however, and this is now, and even then the adulterous friend is distinctly better pleased with himself than Levin. (I know that bit's not in the extract, but you can either look it up or just take my word for it.) The smart move for a latter-day Levin in this situation is just to remind himself that it *is* only a game, and *he* doesn't have to play.

Meanwhile, what's Anna playing at? Although she's going to be a bad girl and betray her husband, she'll do so in a fairly conventional way. She's already one of the most brilliant and admired people in her social circle. So is the dashing Vronsky. The adoration of Vronsky gives her more of that attention which she already knows and enjoys, and which beautiful women were *supposed* to enjoy. Although it's regarded as cheating to engross his attention to the point of sleeping with him, she's still playing basically the same game as her disapproving peers.

2.2.4.2 SWINGING II

Gowan McGland's professional rival is used in this extract by a girl who knows how to make the masculine game work for her. When she tells McGland that the other man is both gay and an inferior poet, she is inviting McGland to assert his own greater manliness on both counts. This girl's trick only works on a man with something to prove *vis-à-vis* his fellow men, but McGland is superlatively such a man.

McGland is not entirely in thrall to the conventional game for men. If he were, then he would be a bit choosier and look for a poetry lover with a better figure – omnivorousness as a sign of desperation can *lose* a man points if he's not careful. So can getting off with a girl who comes on to him before he comes on to her.

As nerds, *we* needn't care about these points. However, we may wonder whether the frantic private game McGland is playing would be any less of a losing game for us than the conventional masculine game.

As for the girl, she's *not* playing the conventional feminine game. She's *not* patiently stimulating the interest of one or more admirers without giving too much away. She's just finding a man she fancies, bonking him and moving on. Her girlfriends might not be impressed by this, but with a figure like hers she's got no status to lose.

2.2.4.3 STUDENT FANTASY II

The girl in Vesna McMaster's poem is playing the conventional game right down the line. Some might object that it is *not* conventional to be quite so vampish, but bear in mind that I'm not talking about conventional *morality*. I'm talking about the game as it is played. At most, this girl is just playing it a bit harder than some.

As for the boy, he's not playing. He's just being played. What *should* his move be? He should walk away. If she's interested in him, then he'll be seeing her again. If, as is more likely, she's having a little game, then he's well out of it.

2.2.4.4 COMING UP ROSES II

We learn in Chris Manby's novel that the too, too exciting Robert is a serial blind dater. With his flattering routine, his big flowers and his fancy car, he does the conventional 'love them and leave them' male game straight down the line. The novel doesn't actually say he cuts notches on his bedhead, but that's probably just because it might give his game away. The only deviation from complete conventionality is that his conquests are acquired through lonely hearts services. Therefore, they would not accrue him as much kudos, other things being equal, as prey trapped in the wild.

For Ruby, similarly, the blind-date context is a deviation from the strictest rules of the conventional female game: it implies a degree of weakness in her 'sensuality for attention' negotiating position from the outset. Awareness of that is reflected in Ruby's initial lack of confidence.

2.2.4.5 SLIPPERY WHEN WET II

The sheer kinkiness of the encounter with Cindy would, in principle, be very good for Martin in the sense of 'Wait 'til I tell the fellas!' However, it so happens that Martin is unlikely to tell the fellas much about this, partly because, after the excerpt quoted, the encounter comes to a deeply humiliating end, and partly because Martin is the novelist's idealised nice guy who wouldn't do that kind of bragging even if it hadn't. (Or at least, he wouldn't do it in direct speech within the pages of the novel.)

Cindy is ostensibly unconventional. She is certainly 'role playing' unconventional. Her unconventionality consists in the fact that she gets attention by flamboyantly knocking off numerous men for real, rather than just by hinting that she might. She remains conventional, however, insofar as attention is what she's after. She goes for a low-status blind date on the assumption that he will be more appreciative – not in the sense of giving her more stuff, like Robert with his expensive roses, but in the sense of paying her more attention.

2.3 Idea 3: Relationship space

Idea 3 covers in more detail a subset of the scope of Ideas 1 and 2. That is, it concerns the 'attention' heading from Idea 1, and the 'conventional female game' from Idea 2.

This idea, 'relationship space', is about that space at the centre of which women (conventionally) want to be.

Hold on tight – steep learning curve ahead! (If you have an allergy to mathematics, then be advised that this section contains traces of nuts.)

2.3.1 Graphs of relationship space

Unlike Idea 1, this idea is not well represented by a 3-D Cartesian diagram. It is better represented using one of those graphs described in that field of mathematics called 'graph theory'. That means it can be defined in terms of 'nodes' (which are typically shown in diagrams as small blobs) and 'edges' (shown as lines connecting one node to another), as per Figure 2.1.

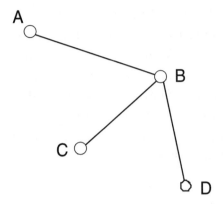

Figure 2.1

It does not matter exactly where each blob is. It does matter which blobs are connected to which other blobs. For example, for practical purposes, Figure 2.2 is exactly the same as Figure 2.1.

In a graph of relationship space, nodes are people, and edges are relationships. So, Figure 2.2 could represent the relationships between a person B and three other people, A, C and D.

2.3.2 How much do you love me? Quantitative attributes of relationships

In the model of human relationships proposed here, each relationship (that is, each 'edge' on the graph) has two important quantities associated with it, which we can call q_1 and q_2:

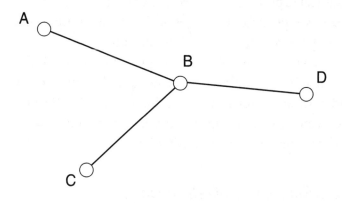

Figure 2.2

q_1 represents the role played by one person in the imagination of another. A larger role is represented by a higher value for q_1. If she can't stop thinking about you, then that's a very high value of q_1.

q_2 represents the immediate presence of one person to another's attention. q_2 can increase as you stand closer to someone. It can also be increased by what you say and the way that you say it. For example, if you say something important which demands a response then this increases q_2.

The bad news is that there are neither the units nor the means for measuring these quantities.

The good news is that we only need to be able to define the 'greater than' relationship and the 'less than' relationship between them, and only in certain circumstances. That being so, the absence of measurement does not give us an insuperable problem. If someone were to find a way to map these two quantities to the set of real numbers, that would be very interesting, but we don't need it.

If you're the sort of nerd who prefers Greek to algebra, then maybe you could call them not q_1 and q_2, but peristasis and epistasis. If you're standing high in a girl's affections, then you're peristatising her. If you're standing heavy on her toes, then you're epistatising her.

2.3.3 Subjectivity of relationships

You will have noticed that the definitions of q_1 and q_2 depend on the point of view of some particular person. For example, suppose that Janet is sitting right behind John. John is obstructing Janet's view of the cinema screen and, coincidentally, daydreaming about Janet. Janet, however, has not recognised John. From Janet's point of view, the relationship with John has a high q_2 and a low q_1, whereas from John's point of view, it has a high q_1 and a low q_2.

In fact, if normal English usage didn't regard two people as having only one relationship with each other at any given time, we might say that they had two distinct relationships, one each.

As an aside, it's worth noting that normal English usage on the subject of human relationships is defined largely by women, they being the ones who mostly use it. It so happens that relationships among women are more likely to be symmetrical (or nearly symmetrical) in respect of q_1 and q_2 than relationships among men. Consequently, women can talk about a relationship *in itself* as being close

or distant, warm or cold, without having to distinguish between the two ends of it.

Be that as it may, when we draw a graph of relationship space, we start with one node, representing one person, and then we add the relationships *of* that person as perceived *by* that person. Values of q_1 and q_2 are shown next to each relationship to which they apply. For example, if we were interested in the point of view of person B, we could start as in Figure 2.3, where x_1 and x_2 represent the values of q_1 and q_2, as perceived by B, in respect of A, y_1 and y_2 represent their values in respect of C and z_1 and z_2 represent them in respect of D.

Restating for the arithmophobes, x_1 tells us how much A peristatises B, x_2 how much A epistatises B, y_1 how much C peristatises B, etc.

If A is in B's face, trying to sell her something, then we can say that x_2 is greater than x_1. If B calls C more often than she calls D then we can say that y_1 is greater than z_1. If, at a particular time, neither C nor D is with B, nor talking to her on the phone, then we can say that y_2 and z_2 are probably both zero. However, if B reads a letter from D, then z_1 can be considered to have a value greater than zero for as long as B's attention is on that letter.

If we then want to take a view about the relationship between, say, A and C, we have two choices:

- either we can start again with a new graph beginning with A or C

- or we can let B *speculate* about the A/C relationship. (If B is a woman, then she is likely to have done this speculation at some time, if only in the back of her mind.)

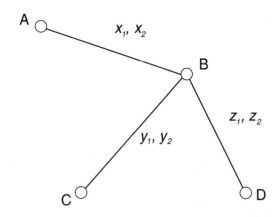

Figure 2.3

If we adopt the second approach, then we can fill out our graph as in Figure 2.4.

However, if A had never met C and D, then the two edges connecting A to C and D would not be present, and α_1, α_2, β_1 and β_2 would be undefined.

On the other hand, we could add still more information to the graph, if B distinguished D's view of C from C's view of D, and if B speculated about how A saw B herself, as distinct from how B sees A.

That would give us what mathematicians call a 'directed' graph, which means that the edges are not just lines but arrows. In our case, each line could be replaced with a pair of arrows, one in each direction, and each arrow would have its values for q_1 and q_2. As well as showing us how much A peristatises and epistatises B, it would also tell us how much B peristatises and epistatises A, and so on.

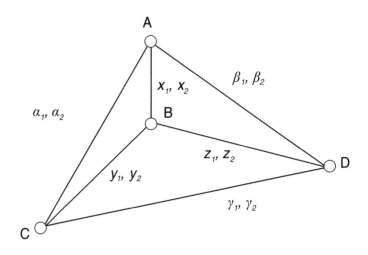

Figure 2.4

This would all look very much like a great mass of lines, with letters and numbers next to them. If you *really* want to see it, please draw it yourself.

2.3.4 Intermission
Well done. You can untwist your tongue now, and might like to take a tea break.

2.3.5 Defining the centre
I wrote earlier that relationship space is the space at the centre of which women conventionally want to be.

It seems from the foregoing that, although each person is always at the centre of their *own* frame of reference, there is no absolute centre of relationship space. Strictly speaking, this is true. However, there are some nodes in relationship space with more edges than others (namely, popular people), and such nodes tend to be connected directly with each other to form clusters where the ratio of edges to nodes is very high.

Furthermore, there are some people (the famous ones) who loom large in the imagination of many others, and the nodes for these people have many edges with high values of q_i, although these edges are not bidirectional, because the famous person has never heard of their individual fans.

Within the set of nodes in relationship space with some direct connection to some particular person, there is often one cluster containing both the greatest q_i values and the highest ratio of edges to nodes. This cluster can be regarded as the absolute centre of the space for all practical purposes. It represents the 'in' crowd.

2.3.6 Why can't people just say what they mean?

This section sets out, as an example, a problem which can be elucidated using the idea of relationship space.

If you are a nerd, then you may well view conversation in terms of the communication of knowledge. You ask people things that seem interesting or important to you and you tell people things which might (you hope) seem interesting or important to them. You realise, as their eyes glaze over, that those particular things don't; but you were trying your best.

For example, suppose that you want to go out with a girl. As a frank and truthful person, you may feel inclined simply to lay this information before her. However, you don't need me to tell you that telling her that you want to go out with her is a counterproductive opening.

Furthermore, even asking her whether she'd like to go out with you, though more polite, is basically a desperate thing to do. It seems that cool men, when they want to go out with a girl, start by saying something to her which includes no mention of 'going out', even though going out is their sole purpose in starting the conversation.

Why do you need to avoid asking the question, or making the statement, that constitutes the whole reason for the conversation? That's the question I'm addressing in this section.

The short answer is that the utterance of a statement or a question can change the quantitative attributes of your relationship with the person you're talking to. You might like to read that again, slowly.

In general, if you talk to someone, then q_2 immediately increases in her view of you. You're epistatising her (a bit). You may also succeed in peristatising her a bit (q_1), but even if you do, this is likely to take time.

Where q_2 exceeds q_1, you are 'in her face' or 'crowding' her, and she does not want you any closer. Where q_1 exceeds q_2, she is interested in you, and she *may* be amenable to getting closer.

The utterance of a statement or question which might be regarded as 'personal' increases your q_2, and if your q_1 isn't high enough to support this, then you're in trouble: hence 'small talk', which creates time for q_1 to rise without raising q_2. Small talk is trivial and irrelevant for a good reason; namely, that if you raise important and relevant issues with someone who doesn't know you very well, then, as well as forcing those *issues* on her attention, you are forcing *yourself* on her attention (whether you meant to or not). This means that q_2 rises and she backs off.

2.3.7 The extracts revisited (again)

There are certain difficulties with illustrating the workings of relationship space by reference to the extracts we've been looking at up to now:

- Most writers most of the time take it for granted that their characters have their q_1s and q_2s in balance. They don't feel they need even to state that this balancing is being done, let alone *how* it is being done. It only becomes visible when, for comic or sinister effect, some nerd is shown doing it wrong.

- The nodes and edges of relationship space are usually filled in gradually over the course of a book, so no single extract shows you much of them.

Nevertheless, here goes.

2.3.7.1 OLD-FASHIONED ROMANCE III

In general, we can say of a lot of nineteenth-century novels that they are set in a particular region of relationship space called 'society' (meaning 'high society'). This region of relationship space has a single great centre in the vicinity of a royal or imperial court. It may have a smaller centre in each English county or Russian province, and it may have yet smaller centres which are local to the salon of some particularly fashionable lady.

Of Anna Karenina in particular, we can say that she started from a fairly central position, as did her lover, but the indiscreet way in which they carried on their affair caused them both to be pushed to peripheral positions. The exact mechanisms involved need not concern us, because they have to do with social conventions which are now obsolete. We can note that one of the things driving Anna to this course was a growing addiction to her own particularly high q_1 value in her lover's eyes.

2.3.7.2 SWINGING III

We might explain the attraction of the girl in the blue wool dress to McGland partly by postulating a desire on her part to get closer to the centre of something (possibly 'the literary world'?), but in this case I think she might have been kidding herself.

2.3.7.3 STUDENT FANTASY III

This is an unusual case in that it is a girl and not a boy who is pushing her q_2 beyond what her q_1 could be expected to bear. She is getting away with it because, whereas most girls know what to do when they find a rude boy in their face, most boys *don't* know what to do with a rude girl. They don't know this precisely because the case *is* unusual.

I'm assuming here that the q_1 is low. That is to say, that this boy has not already been worshipping this girl from afar. If he has, and she knows it, then she really *is* being nasty. In any case, unless the boy wises up, we can be pretty sure that q_1 will rise after this episode, and that this is the girl's intention.

2.3.7.4 COMING UP ROSES III

Knightsbridge represents social centrality (as well as money). Serial-killer hair represents the opposite. (There's a whole other book to be written comparing and contrasting the nerd, who doesn't know how other people feel, with his dark cousin the psychopath, who knows but doesn't care.)

2.3.7.5 SLIPPERY WHEN WET III

Cindy is unusual in that she already lives near enough to the centre of relationship space (by virtue of her famous parents), and she is bored with it. She reminds me of Harold Wilson's complaint that when you finally get to the centre of power (the Prime Minister's office at 10 Downing Street), there's nothing there. It could be argued that the late Princess of Wales had a similar problem.

So instead of wanting, like a conventionally ambitious girl, to be at the centre of the whole world, she wants to be at the centre of one man's private world, if only for a night or two, even if that man is in himself quite boring.

She goes about getting that man's attention on the common assumption that men don't care about relation-ship space. She generates straight q_2 as if following a recipe from a magazine. She subsequently loses it again as the man, Martin, comes to realise over time that, in fact, he does care (though only in the sense of wanting a q_1 connection, not in the sense of wanting to be among the famous).

3 THINGS TO TRY

The previous chapter offered a set of conceptual tools for understanding human sexual behaviour. It described:

- the kinds of things that people feel about sex

- the kinds of things that people conventionally do about it

- how these things bear on people's (especially women's) overall social life and sense of their own identity and dignity.

This chapter uses these tools to explain some things that a nerd can actually do for the benefit of his sex life.

Many nerds don't like taking advice and prefer to work things out for themselves. If that's you, then you may like to skip the rest of this book and just take those tools from Chapter 2 and build your own advice. In that case I thank you for your company up to this point and I wish you all the best.

If you do feel in need of some clearer hints about what to do, then read on, but only after looking carefully at this disclaimer.

People are becoming ever more aware of each other's courtship strategies, so any given strategy is liable to obsolesce as people spot it and think 'I'm not going to fall for that one'. Anyway, women are free individuals, and if she doesn't fancy you, she doesn't fancy you. There are no guarantees of success, only ways to shorten the odds. Life jackets can be found under your seats, and fit over your head like this…

3.1 The collusive relationship

All the advice in this second part of the book could be summed up as follows: as a nerd, you have to sacrifice the thrill of the chase because you're not very good at the chase and won't catch anything. In its place, you must substitute the thrill of collusion. That's the thrill of you and she *contra mundum*.

3.1.1 Why so slow?

Sacrificing the thrill of the chase is necessary for nerds, for this one reason.

If a man with strong social skills makes an inappropriate sexual advance, then he's a loveable rogue. He may get slapped, but he's still a loveable rogue.

If a man with *weak* social skills makes an inappropriate sexual advance, then he's *not* a loveable rogue. *He's* a sinister pervert.

Breathe in. Breathe out. Remember, no one said it would be fair.

3.1.2 What does this 'collusion' involve?

In terms of Idea 1, a collusive relationship involves a lot of work on the attention/intimacy front early on.

In terms of Idea 2, it involves a break from the conventional male game (as already discussed).

In terms of Idea 3, it involves a lot of training and positioning in relationship space before you try anything overtly intimate or sexual.

3.1.3 Where does it get you?

In the end, you and she get to go and be naughty children together.

3.2 How sex joins on to real life

If you don't get much sex, it's easy to see sexuality as somehow divorced from daily reality. It's as if sex happened somewhere else, in a parallel universe. Sex is represented and implied all around us, but never actually experienced. It's a mirage. It feels impossible. It becomes impossible. If you're not careful, you can start seeing sex as being something that only happens in pornography and in bitter and unsettling fantasies. You have to find ways to reconnect sexuality with reality, before you can get into a relationship.

This section follows the pattern set out in section 2.1, 'Idea 1: The space of possibilities'. The basic thesis is that:

- the element of sensuality in sex is not fundamentally separate from sensuality outside sex

- the expression of attention and intimacy in sex is not fundamentally different from expressions of attention and intimacy outside sex

- the pleasures of domination and submission in sex are just the normal, everyday(!) pleasures of domination (or, as it might be, submission), but in a sexual context.

So, you can get the hang of the essential elements of sex without actually having any, and then you just build your relationship out of this handy flat-pack kit. Okay, it's not easy, but at least it gives you a clearer picture of what you have to do.

3.2.1 Sensuality

There's not much about sensuality that a hot bath can't teach you.

People say that there's a great difference between men and women, in that women love to be touched all over, whereas a man cares only about his willy. People say this as though it were a profound and impenetrable mystery.

Lie down in your hot bath, slowly. The water touches you all over. Contemplate how good this feels. Mystery solved.

If we men don't always look for this kind of touch during sex, that's because of things going on *in our heads*. It's not because we physically can't appreciate it.

While you're in the bath, try rolling around a little, to make currents in the water around your body – a sort of 'poor man's jacuzzi'. Maybe you have an actual jacuzzi. Imagine what you might do with your limbs to produce similar sensations in a woman. Okay, that's enough to be getting on with. After all, you'll have to get to know her first.

If you want to know more about sensuality, then you can get used to the practical skills of handling flesh in a 'safe' controlled environment by taking a course in massage. Personally, I'd recommend one with a strong scientific basis in physiology, so you understand more about how bodies (yours and hers) fit together, and what it's safe to do with them. However, there are other styles out there to choose from if you prefer.

So far, I've been talking about touch, but it might help if you took a more voluptuous interest in your food and in the sensations of eating. Also, when you think no one's looking, you could try smelling different varieties of flower and thinking about what people appreciate in them.

3.2.2 Attention

Learn to perform. It doesn't much matter *what* you perform.

The point is, you have to experience the attention of other people as a positive thing. You could try amateur dramatics. You could try music. If all else fails, you could (like many other nerds, including me) try role-playing games.

Create a moment when all eyes are on you. There's an audience, either rooting for you to do something, or appreciating something you've just done. Savour that moment. Like all-over touch, it's one of those pleasures that *real* men aren't supposed to get into. However, like the pleasure of all-over touch, you don't have to be female or gay to get it, and experiencing it can help you get closer to understanding what women want.

If you try this and experience nothing but panic, don't worry. Just try again another time, and keep trying. This exercise is an important precursor to learning to flirt, and you *can* make it work if you practise.

You'll notice that I've only talked here about *receiving* attention, and not about giving it. That's because there's not much that anyone can teach us nerds about *giving* attention. Absolute, devoted attention giving is one of our characteristic skills. We can often be seen about the place giving *total attention* to spotting rare birds, solving higher order differential equations, or stalking and harassing our favourite celebrities.

3.2.3 Power

Don't get too much into this side of things. Courtship strategies based on power are especially difficult and dangerous for nerds, and probably unethical too. However, you should get some feel for how this part of the game is played.

Not many people enjoy being hurt or trapped, but it's quite easy to enjoy being in the presence of something overwhelming, and being carried along by it. Consider, for example, the relationship between, on the one hand, a bungee jumper and, on the other, the force of gravity. That thrill is the socially acceptable analogue to sexual submission. Okay, I'm using my imagination here, but just you try it (bungee jumping, I mean), and then tell me I'm wrong.

The other kind of power thrill is more obvious – that's the one where *you* have the power. Most nerds can find *some* kind of competitive activity where they can actually win sometimes, and that's all there is to it. Failing that, you could just fantasise about winning. Like attention giving (above), it's not something that we nerds need to spend much time working on. We understand it pretty well already.

3.3 Strategic preparation

This section is about things that you can do over the long term to increase your chances with women.

3.3.1 Get a body

Many nerds have a bad relationship with their bodies, regarding them as nothing but a life-support system for a brain, and not a very good one at that.

If you get into the habit of brisk walks to tighten your buttocks and heavy lifting to get some muscle on your chest, it helps you in two ways. First, there's a cosmetic pay-off. By itself, that won't turn you from an unattractive person into an attractive one, but it can help you in the right direction. Second, there's a psychological pay-off. This is probably more important than the cosmetic pay-off. It works on your mind, and it also works on the minds of women.

What it does for your mind is to give you a lift. Once you've got those endogenous morphines flowing after a bit of exercise, life never seems quite so bad. You've got through the pain of the exercise, so you can get through the pain of that last rejection, and keep on going.

What it can do in a woman's mind is subtler, but important. You get a bit of a spring in your step, and somewhere in the back of her mind she gets a tiny, almost homeopathic, dose of thrill. At some subliminal level, you're doing that thing for her which the force of gravity does for the bungee jumper. It's many orders of magnitude smaller, of course, and you can't come up to her on the strength of it and say, 'Fancy a bit of sexual submission?' However, like the cosmetic improvement to your physique, it moves the odds a little bit further in your favour.

3.3.2 Get a persona

Remember that familiar old advice 'just be yourself'? Forget it.

I don't mean you have to abandon your true and inmost self. What I'm talking about is the way you *appear* to be when you're in company. I'm taking it as read that this appearance doesn't always do you justice.

The fact is that most people have what you might call a 'social persona', or maybe more than one. The word persona originally meant 'theatrical mask'. It's a thing you place between yourself and other people, which helps them to understand who you are and what you're doing.

Most people pick up this persona so effortlessly, they don't even know they're doing it. If you are a nerd, then you don't really have a social persona to speak of. That's a drawback, because you need to get a social persona in order to get a social life. However, you have a compensating advantage: unlike many people, you don't just uncritically pick up the personae used by your friends or relations; you have the opportunity to construct one consciously.

3.3.2.1 APPEARANCE AND REALITY

Before I go on, there's a concern I'd like to address, namely that it's dishonest to put a mask between yourself and other people. The thing to bear in mind here is this. Whereas an actual theatrical mask has a real face concealed behind it, which can be seen when the mask is removed, a social persona has no face behind it. Without a social persona, people can barely see *you* at all. (As you may know from experience, this can be very disconcerting for you.)

So, when you work on a social persona you're not concealing a reality, you're making one.

3.3.2.2 THE ELEMENTS OF A PERSONA

A social persona consists of a set of ways of doing certain sorts of things. Broadly speaking, the sorts of things I'm talking about are the sorts of things which bear on the quantitative attributes of your relationships with the people you're talking to; that is, on your q_1s and q_2s (peristasis and epistasis). In particular, you need:

- ways to start a conversation

- ways to end it

- subjects to talk about in between times

- ways to *change* the subject without being rude or abrupt.

All these things can vary between different cultures, subcultures and even individual groups of acquaintances, so I can't make precise recommendations. All I can say is observe how other people achieve those things listed and take note. Note the words, note the tones of voice, and note the body language.

While you're observing, think about how these things relate to q_1 and q_2 (and try not to stare!).

3.3.2.3 HOW TO ACQUIRE THEM

You have to start by identifying techniques and mannerisms in other people and copying them. You have to make sure that, individually, they are not too closely identified with one other person, and that you don't copy all of them from the same person. If you stick to these two principles, then what you're doing won't look too strange.

Once you've got them working, then you will probably want to make changes to them, so as to personalise them. If you have ever worked in software development, then you will be familiar with the practice of copying and then modifying ('tweaking'). This is basically the same.

On the subject of subjects, here's a big *caveat*. You don't sustain a good conversation by being an expert in the subject. That's a recipe for a quarrel or a monologue. Bearing in mind that conversation is the end, and the subject is the means, you should try to learn enough to prompt the other person to talk about whatever *they're* interested in. This basically means you have to learn a little about a lot of things. Unfortunately, the habit of nerds is usually to learn a lot about a few things, or, where we've learned about a lot of things, to share this knowledge uninvited.

3.3.3 Get a look

By 'a look', I mean mostly clothes, though you might also do something about your hair and choice of aftershave. Having been called many things, I can say with confidence:

- that 'poser' is better than 'loser'
- that it's better to be called a wanker because you've put some effort into your image than

to be called one because that really is your
only way to keep the cobwebs off your
dangly bits.

However, don't try to do this bit without advice. You don't
have to take the advice, but there will always be some looks
that just don't suit you, and you want to find this out before
getting humiliated in public.

Also, don't always believe what other males have to say
on the subject. It's not them you're trying to impress
(although, if you can avoid getting beaten up on suspicion
of being a homosexual, that's always a bonus).

3.3.4 Your fellow men

It's a lot easier to get girlfriends if you've got men friends.
This is because of Idea 3. (That was about 'relationship
space', and how women like to be at the centre of it.)

Not all women are equally concerned about being at
the centre of a network of people, but very few would be
happy being entirely disconnected. You don't have to be a
network hub, but you do have to be able to demonstrate a
functioning network connection. If you appear to have no
mates at all, then you might be scary and weird. Also, if
your network only includes other nerds, that might make a
woman nervous.

Remember that principle from Idea 2 – 'What would
my friends say?' Most women do care about what their
friends would say, and you have to respect that. A mixed
social circle is usually fine, but all nerd is a turn-off.

3.3.4.1 BOYS' GAMES

You get to be one of the boys by playing boys' games. Granted, there is the alternative of regular drinking, but that gets expensive and bad for your health. If, like me, you hate sport, just bear in mind that:

- you don't have to play often
- you don't have to play well.

A woman wants to be at the centre, remember, rather than the top. If you're in the game, then you're connected and that's enough. Winning it is not so significant, except to women really preoccupied with power and status, who are probably not for you anyway.

Also, if you do play willingly but badly, then other men won't regard you as a threat. They may regard you as so 'not a threat' that they're willing to be positively helpful in some respects. For example, they can help you with your exercise programme while you're trying to 'get a body' (so you don't put your back out or rupture yourself). Also, they will help you to drown your sorrows after your next rejection. (Unlike regular drinking, this is quite cheap, as you can get drunk quickly, and your health can always recover afterwards.) They may do this kind of thing out of pure kindness, or because they get an ego boost from patronising you. Either way, they're offering something useful, so use it.

However, never forget that when it comes to women you're playing a different game from other men. (Remember Idea 2?) If you go head to head with them, you'll lose. So don't borrow their chat-up lines, nor their girlfriends. Luckily, their girlfriends' friends are another matter.

Note: if you're still a teenager, you may find that the sporty boys are themselves too insecure to tolerate a nerd. In that case, they will just humiliate you and spit you out. The stratagem I've just described gets more feasible as everyone concerned gets more adult. You might have to skip it for now.

3.3.5 Platonic women

I don't mean ideal women, inhabiting Plato's world of Ideal Forms. I mean any females willing to tolerate your company, towards whom you harbour no serious sexual intentions, however desperate you get. This subsection is about how they can help you and therefore, by implication, why you should cultivate them (whether or not you believe that their friendship is its own reward, which it is).

3.3.5.1 NETWORKING

Women have women friends. Some women take pleasure in setting up people with dates, but even if a woman doesn't have this as a hobby, you still get to meet her friends, and she might have said positive things about you.

3.3.5.2 PRACTICAL STYLE CONSULTANCY

Women love men they can go shopping with. If you will make an honest effort to find things to say about what they are thinking of buying, then they will be happy to give you free advice about what might suit you, and why, and what image you might try to project, or might try to avoid projecting.

(If you need some help finding things to say about women's clothes, just think general thoughts about shapes, colours and textures. If you find it really difficult, then spend some time in advance looking at fashion pictures. Describe to yourself the differences between one costume and another, which you like better, and why.)

3.3.5.3 MORAL SUPPORT

If you know that women exist who like you, then that helps you to believe that there's a woman out there somewhere who will fancy you, and belief is important in this game.

3.3.5.4 INSIGHT

When you listen to women talking about men, you can learn things about women that you will never learn from listening to men talking about women. There's a whole different kind of language to learn. As with other languages, the more exposure to it you have, the faster you pick it up. If you want to guess what a woman's thinking, it's much easier if you know the language in which she's thinking it.

3.3.5.5 LEARNING TO FLIRT

What is flirtation, anyway? For a long time, I knew it was something in between normal interaction and foreplay, but couldn't really make sense of it.

Here's a way to understand it. Imagine you and she are holding a length of rope. There's enough tension in this rope to remind you that she's there, but this isn't a tug of war. If either of you wants to get a little closer, you pull a little harder. If either of you feels that's close enough, you pay out some slack.

There are at least two different games you can play with this length of rope. In the more aggressive game, you try to increase the tension smoothly but unexpectedly, so she finds herself pulled towards you before she has the chance to pay out any slack. It has to be smooth, or she just lets go of the rope.

In the more courteous game, you try to read her intentions from the tension in the rope, and respond in the way that most flatters her. So, if she pulls, you move closer. If she pays out, you take up some of the slack (to show that you're still interested in her), but not all of it (to show that you respect her personal space). If she lets go of the rope, you smile modestly, maybe apologise, and put it away for another time.

(There is a third game in the poem 'Sugar-lips'. The girl has tied the boy's rope to the back of her Landrover and is just pulling out of the drive, and I think he should let go now.)

Do not attempt the aggressive game until you feel confident, and do not attempt it at all with your platonic women. The courteous game, on the other hand, is suitable for a wide range of women friends of all ages, and is good practice for non-platonic relationships.

If you can't see how to apply the 'rope' metaphor, it's like this. The tension in the rope corresponds to 'q_1' (from Idea 3, remember?). The length of rope between you corresponds to q_2. You vary the tension mostly by varying the amount of eye contact, but also by other body language cues, like changing the way you're facing, or leaning forward or backward.

If you want to know how the tension in the rope is supposed to feel, then go back to the 'performance' exercise in section 3.2, 'How sex joins on to real life'.

3.3.6 Good persistence and bad persistence

We nerds know how to stick at something once we've made up our minds. Uncharitable people may call this obsessive-compulsive disorder, but we know it's really the virtue of perseverance.

This same characteristic can either help you or hurt you. It's a long road from being a lonely nerd to being half of a happy couple, and you need all your perseverance to get to the end of it.

What you have to avoid is persevering with a particular woman, when she really, really doesn't want you. Even in those jurisdictions where this is not a criminal offence, it will not make you happy. Cut your losses. You may have to cut your losses so many times that you feel like a pollarded oak – a stumpy trunk with no branches left. Remember, though, the oak always grows back.

3.3.6.1 TRUE LOVE, AND HOW TO CURE IT

When you fall in love, you have to remember that this is basically an event inside your head. It is not fair to place any demands on another person just because something inside *you* has blown a fuse.

In fiction, you sometimes read about couples who see each other for the first time and are both smitten. This may happen in real life too. However, it would require a very fortuitous fit between the signals that each person is sending out at the time and the signals that each one deeply wants to receive. I mean the non-verbal signals. As nerds, we have very hit-and-miss non-verbal signals traffic at the best of times, and the chance of it being exactly right at a first meeting, without any preparation, is negligible.

If you find you have very strong feelings about someone before you've got near her, this is a reason *not* to target her as a prospective girlfriend. That's because those very feelings will prevent you from achieving the clear thought and self-discipline which you need to overcome your natural disadvantages.

Romeo had feelings like those, but not for Juliet. Romeo had a terrible crush on someone called Rosaline, which kept him awake at night and made him miserable all day. When Romeo meets Juliet, he's not like that at all. He's attracted to her, but he has enough energy and presence of mind to invent and sustain that clever chat-up line about pilgrimage. Romeo's feelings develop towards their final, suicidal pitch only as Juliet's feelings develop in the same way. 'Romeo and Rosaline', on the other hand, never happened.

If you find yourself (unilaterally) in love, the brutal fact is that you just have to take your mind off it.

First, plan your routine so that you don't see her and, if possible, so that you don't see anything that reminds you of her.

Second, apply your mind to something else. Work will do, though sedentary work is not so effective as physical work. Spending time with other women may help. However, there is a risk that your feelings will just move from one unwitting focus to another.

Remember that these feelings are not a divine inspiration telling you that someone is right for you; they're just parasites on your well-being. Get rid. You'll feel cleaner.

3.4 Tactical preparation

This section is about things you can do to prepare for a particular encounter with womankind.

3.4.1 Tactical goals

Whatever plan you make in respect of a particular woman, it should have the general aim of moving her perception of you through the following stages:

- a – *not unpleasant company*
- b – *more interesting than I thought*
- c – *really nice, actually*
- d – *don't mind if I do.*

It is helpful if, before each encounter with her, you consider which stage you've already reached and whether you're ready to attempt the next stage.

You have to find the right pace for this. Too slow, and you find yourself at stage e – *furniture.* Too fast, and you're at x – *pest.*

Not only do you have to learn, in general, how to make these moves, but also you have to be aware that different women favour different speeds. While you're learning, I recommend erring on the side of 'slow':

- It's possible to recover from *furniture.*

- *Pest* means that you don't just lose her – you also lose her friends and acquaintances.

If you're unsure of what these stages mean, you can think of them as representing increasing degrees of 'peristasis' or 'q_l', as described in Idea 3.

If you're unsure of which one you're at, then ask third parties. Initially, you're likely to be seeing the woman in situations where there are other people present. If you can trust these people, it does no harm to ask them, discreetly, how they think their friend feels about you. This works better with other women, who are delighted to be entrusted by you with what is, in effect, a fresh piece of gossip. With men, beware of wind-ups.

3.4.2 Times and places

Paradoxically, the last place a nerd should go to meet a woman is a place where men conventionally go to meet women. I'm talking about clubs, bars and parties. These environments are set up so as to give maximum exposure to non-verbal skills and instinctive courtship behaviour. In fact, conversation is often drowned out completely, and clear thinking is discouraged by the combination of heavy music and alcohol (or other substances).

Instead, you should concentrate on environments where there's something else to do and something else to talk about. That way, there's less pressure on you and less pressure on her. You can move in and out of flirtation with minimum embarrassment.

Work is not a bad place to start. It's become more dangerous than it used to be because of concerns about harassment. However, harassment only happens if you're pushing your luck. Flirtation on the 'courteous' model never got anyone fired, and it gives a woman plenty of opportunity to indicate whether she'd like you to proceed any further.

Environments where there is a preponderance of women over men may seem like a good idea – dancing classes, for example. However, you may find that both you and they get rather self-conscious, which is bad. Also, you might not be a very good dancer. Drama works better, because you get a mutually supporting 'team' atmosphere in the cast.

3.4.2.1 PLACES TO TAKE HER

When you find someone who might just be amenable to getting to know you better, you have to be very careful about what, exactly, you propose. Supper, for example, is more sexually threatening than lunch. Even coffee can have sexual overtones, as compared to tea.

The question you have to ask yourself, before making your suggestion, is this: will she be able to accept without feeling that she is committing herself, and losing control of the situation? To put it another way, does your suggestion leave her with a clear line of retreat if she has doubts?

3.4.3 Your fellow men (again)

Walking into a room on your own, you stand more risk of looking like a dodgy weirdo than if you walk in with someone else. Of course, in an ideal world, you walk in with a female, so other females get competitive with her, but let's be realistic. Simply not looking downright strange is the priority for us nerds, and a second man can be quite enough for this purpose.

So, for preference, look for activities that you can persuade male acquaintances to do with you. This is not too difficult if they involve drinking at any stage. However, don't make a fool of yourself by trailing around for someone to hold your hand. If getting support is that difficult, just go by yourself.

3.4.4 Look (again)

Don't underestimate the psychological benefits of being showered, shaved and dressed in your best. Some women have said that the trouble someone has taken over their appearance is a turn-on in itself (almost as if that's independent of the actual appearance thereby achieved).

There's an important difference between how you select your wardrobe as a whole (as described in section 3.3, 'Strategic preparation'), and how you select your clothes for a particular occasion. For the former, it is vital to ponder and take advice. For the latter, don't do that. What matters is that you feel confident, and if you spend ages agonising like a girlie over what to wear, that's bad for your confidence. Just pick out something clean and smart, and trust that your original decision to buy it was right.

3.5 Contact

This section is about what happens when you're actually with her (with or without others present).

3.5.1 Staring and personal space

Yet again, we come back to Idea 3. It's natural for us nerds to give our undivided attention to an attractive woman. We do this by facing towards her, leaning towards her, keeping our eyes on her and maybe following her around the room. This is disastrous.

The reason it's disastrous is, in the terms of Idea 3, that it raises q_2 far above the level that any normal level of q_1 can sustain, unless you're already having passionate sex with her by the hour and the two of you have only broken off for a quick breather.

Basically, you have to use non-invasive ways of paying attention. The attention itself is good. Women like it when you can remember every word they've said in the last hour and can ask wise and concerned questions about it all. What you have to change is your body language so that the attention is less obtrusive:

- Be conscious of how close you're standing. Is this closer than other people are standing?

- Be conscious of *how* you're standing. Not only is it intrusive when you thrust your myopic face forwards, but the stooped posture which this promotes is ugly.

- Be conscious of the tension in your face, especially around your eyes. If you're tense, think about something relaxing. For example, think back to that hot bath exercise (section 3.2.1, 'Sensuality'). Also, move your head (by, say, looking around the room), to reduce the tension.

- Be conscious of how and where your eyes are focused. If you realise you've started staring, then an apologetic blink can make all the difference between 'eccentric but nice' and 'stark staring mad'. When she's talking to you, it's quite proper to be looking at her. However, when you reply, you might try focusing into the middle distance, as if to give the deepest possible consideration to your reply. Also, this is a good reflex when you find yourself staring down her cleavage.

• And for goodness sake relax.

You can always look less threatening if you have your head slightly to one side (rather than bolt upright). It's okay to change sides now and again, so you don't get a crick.

Equally, you can always look less threatening if you have a gentle smile on. However, when trying this, you should ask yourself from time to time, 'Do the muscles in my face feel tense?' If so, don't try the smile, because a forced smile is worse than none at all. If feeling pressured, excuse yourself, hide in the toilet and think positive thoughts until your face is your own again. If this toilet has warm water, then rinsing and towelling your face can help.

All of these things could and should be practised, without pressure, when you're doing your 'courteous flirt' thing with your platonic women.

3.5.2 The art of apology

Because you are not very good at reading a woman's signals, you will from time to time find that you have gone too far. You know, q_2 exceeds q_1. When that happens, you have to apologise. Not necessarily at the time (the atmosphere then may be so fraught that you're better off just leaving), but sooner or later, you have to say something. These are the points to remember.

- Find the right idiom in which to apologise. No one knows what q_2 means, but the right substitute varies from one social group to another. To identify the right words, you might try reading the books or magazines she reads and listening to her friends. With luck, you were already doing this kind of thing, before your regrettable incident (whatever it was) occurred.

- Don't be sorry *for yourself*. It ruins the effect; the purpose of the apology is to restore *her* dignity and self-possession.

- Don't expect anything in return for your apology. If you're lucky, you might salvage your reputation. Then again, you might not. In either case, 'sorry' is not a magic word to make her put up with you again.

- Decide in advance how to extricate yourself after delivering the apology. If you don't have an escape plan, then you may find yourself hanging around awkwardly. This may create the impression that you are expecting, say, an immediate reconciliation, which she may not feel like. Just think of something you have to be getting on with and go and get on with it.

- Don't come back in a hurry, unless she makes it *very* clear that she wants you to.

Apologies have to be short and dignified, otherwise they are just painfully embarrassing for everyone. It's better if they are delivered in private, but if she doesn't trust you alone with her any more, then just grit your teeth and apologise in front of whoever happens to be there.

3.5.3 Conversation

Some say it's love that makes the world go round. Some say money. Others say it's angular momentum left over from the process of planetary formation. That third group is overrepresented among the target readership of this book.

We nerds are not very good at conversation. You can't change that, but you can learn to work around it. The basic trick is that, as long as you can keep her talking, you don't *have* to say anything yourself. That way, you only need to have a few interesting things to say, and you can use those things sparingly. Also, by putting her at her ease and making her feel that what she says is important, you can make her think you're 'different from other men' in a positive way, and not just as a euphemism for 'freak'.

3.5.3.1 WE HAVE WAYS OF MAKING HER TALK

If you're worried about how to do this 'prompting her to talk' thing, consider the humble chatterbot. A chatterbot is a computer program which can carry on an online written conversation with a human under the pretence that it too is human. The original chatterbot, ELIZA, was invented in 1966 by Joseph Weizenbaum. It worked by scanning the human's input for words that looked significant, and simply feeding those words back, embedded in open-ended questions. For example, if the most important word in the input seemed to be x, ELIZA might ask something like 'Would you like to tell me more about x?'

According to legend, one of Weizenbaum's female colleagues was testing ELIZA and had to ask Weizenbaum to leave the room because she was so engrossed in this pseudo-conversation that she had started telling ELIZA intimate things about herself.

If you're curious, you can probably find ELIZA's algorithm on the web somewhere, but in any case, it's not that difficult to apply the principle yourself. All that's necessary is that she says *something* to get the ball rolling. Even this you don't always need, provided you know something about her life and concerns from friends, colleagues or previous conversations; then you can just initialise x from one of those sources.

3.5.3.2 IF YOU MUST SAY SOMETHING

Sometimes, prompting her to talk will not be enough, especially if *her* conversational method is to prompt *you* to talk.

If you need to tell her something, then bear in mind what was discussed under section 2.3.6, 'Why can't people just say what they mean?' One of the points in that section was that some statements are implicitly intrusive. They include, but are not limited to, statements about your feelings for her. Fortunately, most statements can be made less intrusive by being wrapped up in some sort of indirection. For example, if you want to inform a girl of a proposition p, then, instead of saying to her, '[p]', you might say 'Allegedly, [p]' or 'It's always seemed to me that [p]', or even, 'What do you think about the idea that [p]?'

A stylised example of this occurs in the famous exchange from the musical *High Society*:

x: Have you heard?

It's in the stars.

Next July we collide with Mars.

y: Well, did you evah?

x: What a swell party this is!

(Excerpt from the song 'Well, Did you Evah' by
Cole Porter. Copyright © Warner/Chappell)

Now, if *x* had said simply 'Next July we collide with Mars', then that would have seemed to demand an urgent practical response (saying goodbye to friends, praying, hiding in the cellar). This would have put a dampener on the conversation. However, by creating a distance between himself and the information, *x* allows *y* to consider the information as a conversation piece, without feeling pressurised by it.

Note that this 'wrapping' process doesn't require you to disavow the information. You can say something like 'Some people say that [*p*], and I believe it'. It just means that you're giving the person you're talking to an option as to whether to take on board the full implications of *p* or not.

Of course, there are propositions which, if true, really do require people to take on board their practical implications – for example: 'I love you'; 'global capitalism is destroying the Earth's ecosystem'; 'aliens have infiltrated the government'; or 'Jesus is alive'. If you believe one or more of these propositions to be true, then you are quite right to try to bring them to the attention of the relevant people. However, once you do so, you are no longer in the business of getting better acquainted with those people, and have instead embarked on an entirely different sort of project, namely the project of trying to turn their lives upside down. It might be prudent to get to know them first.

3.5.3.3 YOUR INTERESTS

If asked, you should not try to hide what your interests are, even if you know that most people find them profoundly dull. However, what you must do is find appropriate ways of referring to them. There are three principles to bear in mind here.

First, you should refer to your interests using the same terminology as people who are not interested in that interest. For instance, you may be a railway enthusiast, but you know in your heart that other people's word for it is 'trainspotter'. So, say trainspotter. Say it with an ironic smile if you like, but say it.

The second is that defending or justifying a 'boring' job or hobby is counterproductive. You may happen to know that the pursuits of the railway enthusiast are actually more interesting, more intellectually stimulating, maybe even nobler, than some other more glamorised pursuits you could mention. You may be right. I'm not taking issue with that view. However, if you put that view, unprompted, to the women you're attracted to, then you're going to stay single a little longer.

The third is that detail is bad, unless specifically requested. If you've ever tried to present a technical idea to your non-technical manager, then you know the kind of thing I'm talking about. Whatever you're doing in your job or hobby can always be presented as an instance of something more general, more abstract all right, something vaguer. It goes against the grain for a nerd to be vague, but in love, vague is good – vague is mysterious. For example, if you're working on protocol stacks, say 'computer networks'. If she wants to know more, she can ask.

If she does ask, and you want to tell her something, but feel she might not be ready for the full technical story, then consider this. Almost any technical task or problem, however obscure, can ultimately be traced back to some human factor. At the end of the day, it's about some person or group of people trying to achieve some goal. That's why the technology is there. No, really, it is. If you answer queries by talking about this human factor, then what you're doing will sound much more interesting to outsiders, especially females.

Even if you observe all these three principles, you may still find that, after owning up to whatever it is you do, you're faced with a nervous reaction, or an inclination on a woman's part to back away. To get out of this mess, all you have to do is pass the conversational ball back to her as quickly as possible. Just ask her something about what *she's* interested in, and she'll probably forgive you your eccentricity. Given time, she may even try to learn about it properly. If she does that, you know you're well away.

3.5.3.4 PAYING COMPLIMENTS

Women are wonderful. Even if a woman did nothing at all, it would still be better to have her in the room with you than not, because, bluntly, women smell nicer than we do. Moreover, most women can, in addition, actually do things:

- They can endure more physical hardship than we can, but they are still soft to the touch.

- They can see directly a whole world of social relations that we can barely infer (on a good day they can, anyway).
- They can fit more distinct tasks into each day, on less sleep, than we can.

Amazingly, in spite of all this, they still care what we think of them and appreciate reassurance from us, in one form or another.

Any particular woman may have her own particular splendours as well, but in any case, with almost any woman, you should be able to say with complete honesty that it's nice to see her and you hope she's well.

When you first feel you've won enough trust to move on from generalised pleasantries to more personal remarks, you're better off complimenting something the woman has *done* than something she was born with. For example, you might observe that her choice of top emphasises the colour of her hair nicely. This is better than just telling her she's got very nice hair, because it means you are imaginatively entering into her life and trying to look at her choices from her point of view.

To put it in the high poetic language of Idea 3, you are raising the values of q_1 between you and her. If, on the other hand, you just tell her she has a nice [body part], then that's all q_2 and very little q_1.

If really stuck on the question of what sort of compliment to pay, then consider this tip from the eighteenth-century rotter the Earl of Chesterfield:

Women who are either indisputably beautiful, or indisputably ugly, are best flattered upon the score of their understandings; but those who are in a state of mediocrity, are best flattered upon their beauty, or at least their graces; for every woman, who is not absolutely ugly, thinks herself handsome; but not hearing often that she is so, is the more grateful, and the more obliged to the few who tell her so; whereas a decided and conscious beauty looks upon every tribute paid to her beauty only as her due; but wants to shine, and to be considered on the side of her understanding; and a woman who is ugly enough to know that she is so, knows that she has nothing left for it but her understanding, which is consequently (and probably in more senses than one) her weak side. But these are secrets, which you must keep inviolably, if you would not, like Orpheus, be torn to pieces by the whole sex. (Chesterfield 1774)

Rather like Machiavelli, Chesterfield is morally repugnant but makes astute observations and makes them clearly.

3.5.3.5 TRUTH AND HONESTY

Mark Twain said of the young George Washington: 'He was ignorant of the commonest accomplishments of youth. He could not even lie.' If you are a nerd, then you may well find yourself labouring under a similar disability. Because we nerds find it hard enough to communicate our actual feelings, we find it more or less impossible to convey fake feelings successfully.

In practical terms, you have to start believing that she is special and that her happiness is your concern. This is a fairly simple positive-thinking exercise. You just have to remember:

- not to talk yourself into a unilateral crush on her

- not to kid yourself that your sincere concern gives you any rights over her.

3.5.4 Your feelings, considered from a tactical point of view

It's important to demonstrate emotional literacy by participating in discussions of *her* feelings, or of people's feelings in general, but it can be equally important to be a bit reticent about your own. Women will say they like a man who can talk about his feelings, but you shouldn't take this at face value.

First of all, if you talk about yourself too much from any point of view, even the emotional, then you're boring, and furthermore you're being 'a typical male'. Second, when you volunteer information about your emotional life, you risk becoming the man that she likes to have as a friend, but wouldn't think of in a sexual way. While this is better than nothing, you don't want all your prospects to turn out this way.

Why is that? Well, I think it's like this. You should be coy about giving away too much of your inner life for exactly the same reason as girls are sometimes coy about their bodies. When you've exposed all your needs and vulnerabilities to a girl, then, to all intents and purposes, she's already had you. Unless she has strong reasons to want you for your body, or your fame or money or status, you've blown it.

On the other hand, if you only give away hints about your deeper self, then the girl can persuade herself that you're much deeper than you actually are; and wiser, for that matter. It's like the way that you imagine covered breasts to be rather larger and shapelier than they turn out to be when uncovered.

So you see, women will say they like men to show their feelings in much the same way as men will say, if asked, that they like women to show their breasts. It doesn't make showing them a good strategy. (Mind you, once you've got a functioning sexual relationship, the rules change. Emotional frankness becomes a good thing. It's just when you're still aspiring to that condition that you have to be more careful.)

3.5.5 *The last mile*

This section is about the final stage of transforming yourself from friend to boyfriend. Without a good instinct for how the woman feels, this is like trying to land a plane without instruments. Are you coming in too steep or too shallow? What's your speed? Is there enough runway? Are you, in fact, at the right airport?

It can be done, but you really don't want to rush it. The consequences of getting it wrong are too ugly. If in doubt, pull up, circle, and try again later.

(Supply your own 'undercarriage' joke here.)

3.5.5.1 THE RETURN OF CAPTAIN CAVEMAN

The main thing about this 'last mile' stage is that you have to become masculine again. Up to this point, you've been bending over backwards to meet a woman on her own terms and talk to her in her own language. Remember, though, that getting in touch with your feminine side is not the final object of the exercise. What you're trying to do is get in touch with *her* feminine side.

To make the transition to being someone exciting, you have to do a little work on that 'power' thing discussed in Idea 1. That doesn't mean you start behaving like a domineering person who's going to impose his will on her. Some women might like that, but let's not go there. I'm talking about some demonstration that time spent with you would not be boring.

Achievement, of some sort, often supplies this demonstration. It's a common mistake for nerds to believe that high achievement is a *substitute* for all the work with women you've been doing so far. Those men go on to become the 'successful businessmen' who litter the lonely hearts columns. Achievement is not a substitute for getting close to women, but it is a useful adjunct.

If achievement is used as an adjunct to intimacy and not a substitute, then it doesn't have to be very high. Bill Gates had to become the richest man in the world before a woman would look at him. For you, it may be enough just to win third prize in the pub darts competition out of a field of four. That's if you've done the groundwork, so that your woman is rooting for you anyway, and if you share it with her and make it *feel* like a success.

3.5.5.2 HEARTBEAT

To put it at its crudest, what you're trying to achieve with all this rediscovered masculinity is a simple physiological effect in your woman, namely an increased pulse rate. You've already established that she likes you and trusts you. You just have to make it that she's excited about you. In the first instance, she just has to be excited about *something*, and you have to be there at the time. There's plenty of time to get her excited about you in particular further down the line.

One thing you have to avoid, though, is lunging at the first sign of a glint in her eye. You might have been wrong about the glint and, even if you were right that she was excited, she might not yet have made the hoped-for connection between her excitement and you. In either of these cases, once you've lunged, the only way she can express herself is by a humiliating physical response, like brushing you off or turning away. Neither of you wants that to happen.

So, what can you do once the glint tells you you've achieved the heartbeat thing? Ask her for a proper date.

3.5.5.3 JUST THE TWO OF YOU

At this point, you have to pick your words with particular care. For example, suppose you ask, 'Will you be my girlfriend?' 'Yes' could, in some circumstances, be taken to mean: 'I hereby undertake to offer sexual favours on demand, to launder your underwear and to abstain from the company of my other male friends, until further notice.' You may not mean it like that, but she doesn't know you don't, so she's going to say 'No'.

Note: don't try to avoid this issue by spelling out what you do mean; that feels to her all the more like negotiating a binding contract, which feels like a trap, and anyhow, it's weird.

I know it goes against our nerdy instincts to leave things deliberately ambiguous and undefined, but that's how it has to be. The reason it has to be that way is that spelling things out implies things about the power relationship between you and her, and brings that power relationship to the fore. Unless she's an out and out sadomasochist, the relationship will work much better if the 'power' aspect is left in the background, so that *both* of you feel you have an adequate degree of control over what's going on.

So, don't say 'proper date'. Even at this stage, that's a bit on the crass side. What you have to do is propose something to her which, she will understand, is likely to mean your hands on some part of her by the end of the evening. It might be a candlelit dinner, a late film or private view of your etchings. The point is that, in responding, she can give you her feelings about the idea of you touching her, and she can do this in such a way that neither of you gets humiliated.

Choosing which proposition to put to her is the tricky bit here, and it's one of the many areas in which other female friends can be helpful. You can say something like 'Can you keep a secret? I'd like to ask so-and-so to do something romantic, and I'm thinking of suggesting such-and-such. What do you think? Would that be appropriate?'

Immediately, the forces of gossip are on your side. You might find that your intended woman has been fore-warned, but that's actually a good thing, because the last thing you want to do is suddenly spring on her something that might damage your friendship. The best bit is that, even if she decides she doesn't fancy you, the word is out that you're not as cold a fish as you look, and that may help to get you the attention of the *next* woman.

Come the date, you're really playing the same kind of flirting game that you've been practising all along, but with a shorter length of rope. A little gift is good, especially a carefully chosen gift which shows how much you've learned about her. From there on in, you're in her hands, you lucky thing.

3.6 No, actual contact

There are lots of places where you can learn about particular sexual techniques. There are magazines you can read. There are videos you can watch. I don't intend to duplicate that material. If you have read how to strip down, clean and reassemble a woman's genitals while blindfolded, that's all to the good, but it's not what I'm going to talk about here.

When you touch a woman, it's important to 'know what you're doing'. However, 'knowing what you're doing' does not mean being in possession of a particular body of information. It means being in possession of a particular state of mind. It's about two things, namely confidence and decisiveness.

3.6.1 Confidence

You can increase your confidence by knowing, from all your preparatory work, that this woman is basically amenable to what you're about to do.

You can increase your confidence by remembering those things you've learned about what can feel good to *you*. She's not really so different.

Don't worry too much about things like erogenous zones. Any part of the body with a lot of nerve endings can get excited. A woman has most of her nerve endings in the same places as you have yours – anywhere you're ticklish, really. Furthermore, any part of the body with fewer nerve endings can also get excited. You just have to be a little firmer.

3.6.2 Decisiveness

Whenever you put your hand on her body, you have to know in advance where it's going. Otherwise, the experience for her is just ticklish and faintly creepy. How do you decide in advance what to do next?

Try having a metaphor. I mean, try thinking about something you know you're good at, and relating your feelings about that to what you're doing with your woman. Actually, it doesn't even have to be something you're really good at. It could just be something you could imagine you're good at.

Imagine you're playing music on her body, or that you're painting a picture on her, or telling a story on her. It could be any kind of thing, as long as it's some kind of thing that has a structure that you can feel confident with. It could be an elegant mathematical proof, if that's your most natural experience of beauty.

This may seem weird, but *she* doesn't have to be aware that that back-handed pass over her nipple is really a lemma, and that thing you're doing in her hair is a footnote. All she experiences is the feeling that you're somehow in your element, even though, in fact, you've never done this stuff before in your life.

3.6.3 Herself in particular

There is a pay-off from all the attention you've been giving her before you ever got to touch her. It has given you a chance to work out what her preferences might be in the terms of Idea 1. You know, is she into slow, wallowing sensuality? Would she like to play games to keep your full attention on her? Would she be more excited if you lifted her up and took her without much warning?

It ought to be possible to make some guesses about these things by observing her non-sexual behaviour which you've been doing patiently for some time now. (If you can't work out the connections, you might like to go back to section 3.2, 'How sex joins on to real life'.)

Having made some guesses on this subject, you can adapt your approach. A sensualist might like to combine sex with a rich meal, a scented candle, a bath or a massage. A real flirt might prefer a game of strip poker.

If she's into the 'having power' thing, then you don't need my suggestions – *she* can tell you. The other end of the 'power' spectrum can be handled by a little modulation of the way in which you normally touch her. Continuous contact relaxes, discontinuous contact stimulates. Spanking is like stroking, only very, very discontinuous.

3.6.4 Colluding again

Remember that ideal of the 'collusive relationship'? That plays a big part in managing your physical contact. If your relationship is collusive enough, then you don't have to flounder around trying to guess her feelings and intentions. You can look her straight in the eye and ask her how she would feel about:

- 'holding hands?' or

- 'having your neck kissed?', or as it might be

- 'bending over that sideboard while I shag you until my penis falls off?'

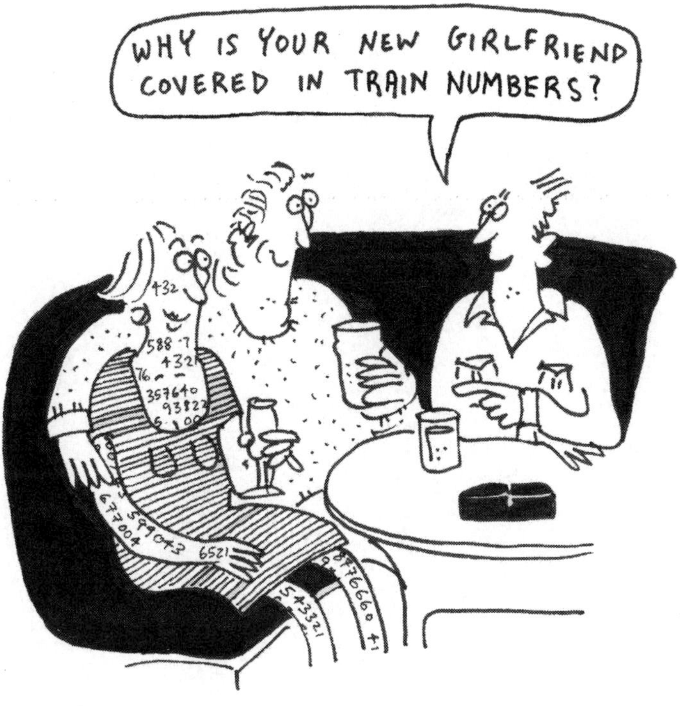
WHY IS YOUR NEW GIRLFRIEND COVERED IN TRAIN NUMBERS?

Furthermore, *she* can look *you* straight in the eye and tell you that sideboard has a knobbly edge and a wobbly leg and she doesn't like the look of it. This sofa, on the other hand…

4 AFTERWORD

Cigarette?

Seriously – hope, pray and never give up. Every dog has his day.

5 APPENDIX: SOME SUPPLEMENTARY THOUGHTS

This Appendix is not the solution to any known problem. It dangles here to entertain those people who, like me, enjoy books and ideas for their own sake. I picture such people batting it back and forth like kittens with a Christmas decoration, under the disdainful noses of normal people.

5.1 Theoretical context

It's all very well in practice, this book, but does it work in theory? The actual conclusion of the book is simply a sexual relationship established by a hypothetical nerdy man. However, the way in which that pragmatic, material conclusion is reached implies some other conclusions bearing on fields including philosophy and psychoanalysis.

5.1.1 Philosophy

For the sake of simplicity, I am going to take one book to stand for current trends in philosophy, namely Richard Rorty's (1989) book *Contingency, Irony and Solidarity* (not all that current, I admit, but it will have to do – it's post-modernist and fairly accessible). That book rejects the idea of a 'privileged meta-narrative' as being oppressive. (A 'meta-narrative' is something which places some ordinary narrative about the world into a wider system. A 'privileged meta-narrative' is one that aspires to be the last word on the subject, on the grounds that it directly reflects a reality underlying those other narratives.)

My book bucks this trend by proposing a meta-narrative, but makes this compromise with the trend: I offer no absolute *a priori* grounds for ascribing privilege to that meta-narrative, except insofar as it 'works', and solves things that can be agreed to be problems. In this respect, I am claiming the same kind of status within the post-modern worldview that science has. However, my book is not scientific. It's not scientific, because it offers no new facts. Instead, it's philosophical, in the sense that it rearranges facts you already knew in such a way as to make sense of them.

And it's not post-modernist, because the post-modern environment described by Rorty revolves around a series of social interactions with no reference beyond themselves, and with no overarching logical system. The trouble with that environment is that it's very hostile to nerds although, at the philosophical level, it doesn't yet know that it is.

5.1.2 *Psychoanalysis*

What I am about to say involves a crass simplification of what Freud said. In particular, I am ignoring *thanatos* to focus entirely on *eros*. My excuse is that I am writing about what our society's collective memory thinks Freud said, not what he actually said (which was, in general, rather more sensible).

In the analytical field, my conclusions reverse the explanatory direction of Freud; whereas, as popularly understood, Freud explained everything else in terms of sex, I have explained sex in terms of everything else. The reason for this is very simple: in any kind of explanation, if the *explanans* is not initially understood better than (or at least as well as) the *explanandum*, then the explanation is a waste of breath. So, Freud's way of explaining things is only sensible for people who understand sex better than they understand anything else. Such people may exist, but not among Aspergers.

5.2 Cartesian diagrams of the space of possibilities

Gentle reader, Figure 5.1 is a picture of a standard X-Y-Z space for use in three-dimensional Cartesian diagrams. X is the direction from left to right, Y is the direction away from you, and Z is the direction up the page. That little 'x-marks-the-spot' in the middle is called the origin. Those things like overlapping panes of tinted glass represent the planes which intersect at the origin, labelled as the XY plane (that's the horizontal one), the XZ plane and the YZ plane.

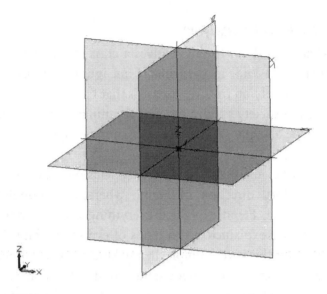

Figure 5.1

In all the diagrams in this Appendix, the Z axis represents sensuality, the Y axis attention, and the X axis power. Because I can't imagine any such thing as 'less than zero sensuality', the XY plane (where Z equals zero) constitutes a sort of floor, below which we won't be seeing much action. (I suppose you might consider pain or discomfort as indicating negative sensuality, but my hunch is that where they are involved in sexual pleasure at all, it's primarily for reasons to do with power relations.)

Negative X and Y, however, are defined. Negative X represents the submissive end of the spectrum of power thrills (so those experiences are happening towards the left-hand side of the page), while positive X represents the dominant end.

Negative Y represents the thrill of receiving attention, so that experience is the part that you can imagine projecting out of the page towards you (where are those 3-D glasses when you need them?), whereas positive Y represents the giving of attention, into the depth of the page, as it were. Don't worry – the cute symbolism of the Y axis, in both directions, is just a coincidence.

5.2.1 Old-fashioned romance

In Figure 5.2, the vaguely saucer-shaped object represents the early interaction between Anna Karenina and Count Vronsky. Sensuality is barely above zero at that stage, but they're both strong, impressive people, and sizing each other up in those terms from the beginning. The shape is symmetrical in the YZ plane because, though neither is submissive to the other, each is attracted by the other's power. It's symmetrical in the XZ plane because they see eye to eye. I think a lot of the strength of their mutual attraction lies in their being evenly matched socially and psychologically. That's what you're seeing in the approximately circular shape I've drawn for them.

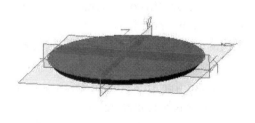

Figure 5.2

As the story progresses, their affair swells into that shown in Figure 5.3). Because it's a Romance, with a capital R, the lovers only need one shape between them to contain the whole of their experience.

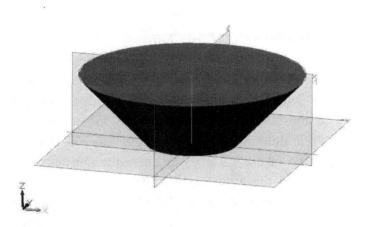

Figure 5.3

5.2.2 Swinging

Now we can contrast this with the little encounter in section 2.1.3, 'Swinging'. Here it is, shown in Figure 5.4. The obvious thing about this one is that there are two quite distinct experiences, his and hers.

His is the one in the near right-hand quadrant, hers the one in the far left-hand quadrant.

We can speculate that this sort of arrangement is more common than the 'high romantic' arrangement, because there's obvious complementarity between, for example, liking to pay attention and liking to receive it. This is just a case of 'opposites attract'.

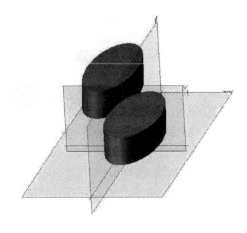

Figure 5.4

I've drawn the two shapes floating above the XY plane, not resting on it, because I don't think there's any point in the passage I quoted when sensuality is far from the mind of either party. However, unlike the sensuality of Anna Karenina and Vronsky, which feeds off the other aspects of their relationship, the sensuality of Gowan McGland and his literary groupie is just 'there', and shows no signs of development. Hence, no tapering of the shapes in the McGland diagram.

5.2.3 Student fantasy

The experiences of Anna Karenina and her lover were gloriously united. The experiences of Gowan McGland and his one-night stand were conveniently complementary. Now, what have we got here?

In 'Sugar-lips' (Figure 5.5), not only are the 'his and hers' experiences not shared, they are not even balanced.

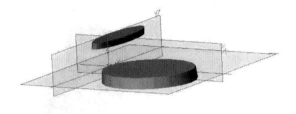

Figure 5.5

This time, it's the girl who's in the near right-hand quadrant, enjoying power and at the centre of attention. I've drawn her shape resting on the XY plane on the assumption that most of the sensual imagery of the poem refers to things that she is suggesting in his head, and her main satisfaction comes from her ability to reach into his head. For her, the cherry is just a cherry.

Now look at his sad little ellipse, pressed up against the YZ plane. Though he is being dominated, there's nothing to suggest that he enjoys this much (unless he's so jaded that he'd enjoy being mugged); he just can't stop looking. What he sees lifts him off the floor sensually but doesn't take him very high; it's a thin sort of thrill.

5.2.4 Coming up roses

This is a different kind of mismatch, arising from deception (Figure 5.6). This time the woman, Ruby, is mostly in the near left-hand quadrant (happily believing that she has the

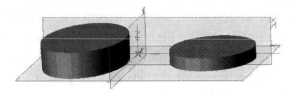

Figure 5.6

sincere attention of a powerful man). She overlaps into the far left-hand quadrant insofar as she enjoys his looks as well as his confidence and credit card.

So far, this is a classic feminine position, in the tradition of 'Some day my prince will come, sweep me off my feet and love me for ever after'. The trouble is, her Robert is not really in the complementary far right-hand quadrant ('You have captured my heart and I will adore, cherish, guide, protect and fund you for ever'). He's just pretending to be. That clear space between him and the YZ plane shows you how manipulative he is, and his token little overlap beyond the XZ plane shows you how self-regarding. I don't think he even enjoys her much sensually (until later, when he gets her into bed) – whereas her sensuality is engaged from an early stage, partly thanks to a rich (but sadly deluded) imagination.

5.3 Suggested para-academic research

I'm not an academic, nor a director of research. I have no grants to allocate nor graduate students to task. However, I offer some lines of enquiry which might be interesting as marginal activities or skunkworks for people better qualified than myself.

5.3.1 Para-academic?

Just in case you're curious, I coined the word 'para-academic' by analogy with 'paramilitary':

- Paramilitaries have all the fun of playing around with guns without the tedious accountability of real soldiers. (In much the same way, I never had to get this book peer reviewed.)

- Paramilitaries, if they make a nuisance of themselves for long enough, sometimes get incorporated into regular armed forces, with an amnesty for what they might have got up to in the past. (I don't know whether, in real life, anyone's ever been offered a research job on the basis of, say, things they contributed to Wikipedia, but I bet it will happen one day.)

5.3.2 Numbers for the graphs

Both in section 2.3.2, 'How much do you love me? Quantitative attributes of relationships', and in the Cartesian diagram examples, there's a conspicuous lack of numbers. This lack makes both these parts of the book semantically ambiguous. They're good enough, I hope, to support the central purpose of the book and be helpful to nerds, but without numbers (or at least, some definition of a possible source of numbers) they won't do as Science.

So, here's a para-academic project for anyone who might like them to be science: find measurable things that correspond to the postulated quantities in those parts of the book.

5.3.2.1 NUMBERS FOR RELATIONSHIP SPACE

This section is about finding numbers for q_1 and q_2. It might be easiest to start with q_2, because q_2 is more directly observable by third parties. For example, you could in theory whip out a tailor's tape measure at any time to measure how close one person is standing to another. You might want to use a more discreet technology, because leaping in with a tape measure would itself be a high q_2 intervention, and would disrupt the system you're trying to observe. However, my point is that simple spatial measurement would give you part of what you need here. Unfortunately, it won't give you all you need, because there are other factors besides distance which influence how much one person impinges on another – staring from a distance, for example, can be more intrusive than modestly standing by.

The difference between q_1 and q_2 is largely to do with the difference between being present to someone's imagination and being present to their senses. To make it easy for ourselves, we might start by restricting ourselves to the sense of sight. For example, experiments have been done in the past using a sort of visor which can detect where the wearer's eyes are focused. If this technology could be miniaturised to the point where it was discreet, and combined with simple video capture, then we could record (through the video capture) how much of a person's field of view was occupied by another person, and (through the 'visor', perhaps now in the form of sunglasses) how much of the time the eyes were focused on that person. You can imagine more than one way in which those two bodies of data could be combined to produce a number.

Then to this data we would have to add some language processing, so as to take account of intrusive or attention-grabbing language (as well as volume of speech, of course). After doing language, we'd have to do body language (how a person is standing, not just where they're standing – where their eyes are focused, for example). Then we'd want to be able to quantify smells, such as intrusive aftershave.

Having established ways to harvest these different kinds of data, we'd need a way to integrate them, by reference to their effect on brain activity. If we could identify a particular form of brain activity which varied only in quantity between an aftershave response, a visual response and a linguistic response, and which differed quantitatively between, for example, different quantities of aftershave, then we'd have a reference point for q_2. I understand how big an 'if' that is, and I suspect that it would not be enough just to measure how intensely a particular brain region 'lights up'. Something more abstract would be required, but it would take a proper neuroscientist to guess what.

In case that's not challenging enough, let's consider how to measure q_1. This job is entirely inside the brain. Suppose that we can identify regions of the brain used in memory, in planning or in daydreaming. The challenge would be to identify and measure the content of those memories, plans or daydreams, so that we know not only who is in them, but also how prevalent a given person is in them, compared to other content.

I guess that the way to measure this would be indirect. It might involve showing subjects a number of unrelated people, including some that they know to varying degrees and others that they don't know, and seeing what brain responses vary, and by how much, and, out of all that data, somehow sifting one variable scalar parameter – and that would be q_1.

If, miraculously, we were able to come up with good candidate metrics for q_1 and q_2, we could validate them with some anthropology whereby we would try to identify common tolerable ratios of q_2:q_1 for a given culture or sub-culture, and we might then feed back the anthropological data into a refinement of our definition of the metrics.

5.3.2.2 NUMBERS FOR THE SPACE OF POSSIBILITIES

This section is about finding numbers for the axes of those diagrams which you can find earlier in this Appendix.

So, we just have to find a variable that measures sensuality, a variable that measures interpersonal power and a variable that measures the giving and receiving of attention. Oh yes, and they ought to be orthogonal to each other.

After all those suggestions for quantifying q_1 and q_2, I have left this as an exercise for the reader. You weren't busy today, were you?

REFERENCES

Note

Regarding the Chesterfield and Tolstoy references, I now forget which edition or translation I have quoted in this book, and from which pages. I apologise to the serious scholar for this lapse.

Chesterfield, Earl of (1774) *Letters to his Son on the Art of Becoming a Man of the World and a Gentleman.*

De Vries, P. (1984) *Reuben, Reuben.* Harmondsworth: Penguin, pp.200, 202.

Manby, C. (2002) *Getting Personal.* London: Hodder, pp.168–169, 205–207, 225–226.

McMaster, V. (1993) 'Sugar-lips.' In M. Graham, S. Heaney and R. James (eds) *The May Anthology of Oxford and Cambridge Poetry,* Cherwell: Varsity.

Rorty, R. (1989) *Contingency, Irony and Solidarity.* Cambridge: Cambridge University Press.

Tolstoy, L. (1878) *Anna Karenina.*